I Can Count

By Carl Memling

Pictures by Feodor Rojankovsky

MERRIGOLD PRESS • NEW YORK

See, feed and count all the zoo animals.

I can count.

So can you.

So let's count

What's at this zoo.

1

ONE wet hippo coming up for air.

TWO snapping alligators—I do declare!

3

THREE thin giraffes

too

tall

for

their

stall.

FOUR hungry lions roaring by the wall.

FIVE frisky monkeys—my, what tricks!

Now count the kangaroos with care.

One, two, three, four, five, and
Baby Kangaroo makes **SIX**.

1, 2

One, two,
Come to the zoo.

3, 4

Three, four,
Lions roar.

5, 6

Five, six,
Monkey tricks.

I can count
From one to six.
And so can you.
But are we through
With this zoo?

No!

7

SEVEN big elephants.
Last one gets a nut.

EIGHT shaggy buffalos.

8

Last one gets a butt.

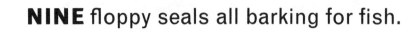
NINE floppy seals all barking for fish.

9

10

TEN tawny tigers,

   their tails going swish, swish, swish.

I can count:

1 wet hippo

2 snapping alligators

3 thin giraffes

4 hungry lions

5 frisky monkeys

6 kangaroos

7 big elephants

8 shaggy buffalos

9 floppy seals

10 tawny tigers.

And so can you.

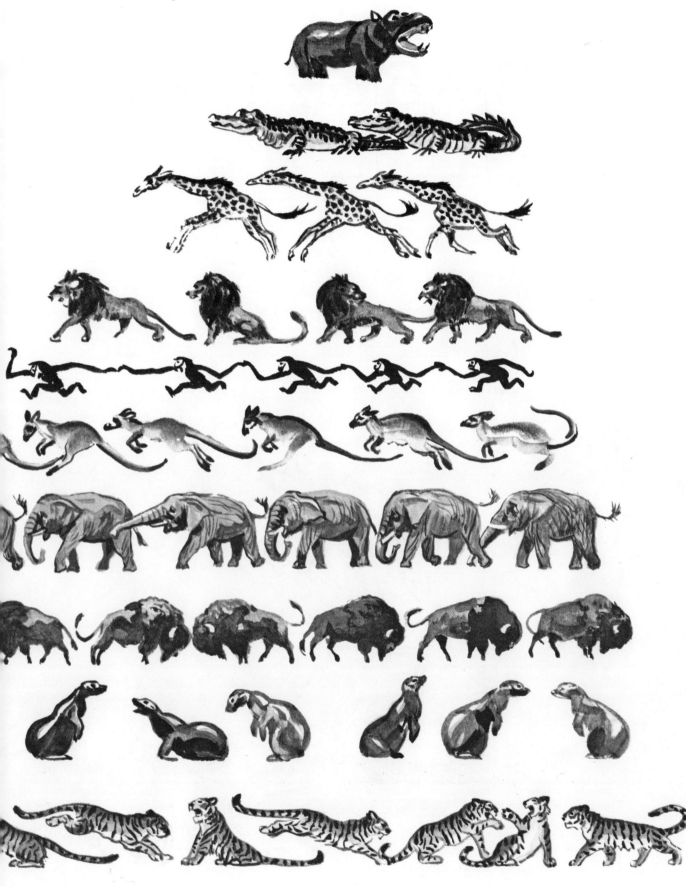

I can write them, too.

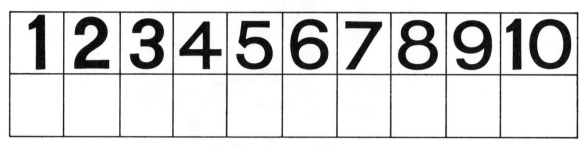

1	2	3	4	5	6	7	8	9	10

We are through

With this zoo.

We can count from one to ten.

Now let's go home,

And start all over again.